Mentoring 101 - Your Guide to Mentoring Student Teachers with Confidence

Quick Reads for Busy Educators

Cheryl Angst

Published by Cheryl Angst, 2023.

MENTORING 101 - YOUR GUIDE TO MENTORING STUDENT TEACHERS WITH CONFIDENCE

First edition. June 3, 2023.

Copyright © 2023 Cheryl Angst.

ISBN: 979-8223829850

Written by Cheryl Angst.

Also by Cheryl Angst

Quick Reads for Busy Educators
Gamifying Education - How to Engage and Motivate Students Through Games
Unlocking Gamification - Exploring the Impact and Importance in Education
Winning in the Classroom - Using Bartle's Gaming Styles to Empower Learners
Who Packed Your Parachute? Why Multiple Attempts on Assessments Matter
The Power of Discussion - A Guide to Using Literature Circles in the Classroom
Together We Teach - Transforming Education Through Co-Teaching
Mentoring 101 - Your Guide to Mentoring Student Teachers with Confidence

Table of Contents

Dear Reader,

Welcome to the extraordinary world of mentoring! It is with great joy and anticipation that I extend my warmest greetings to you as we embark on this incredible journey together. Within the pages of this book, we will explore the depth and richness of the mentoring experience, unlocking the potential for profound growth and transformation in the lives of our student teachers.

Mentoring is a sacred bond, a relationship built on trust, support, and shared aspirations. As a mentor, you have the unique privilege of guiding and shaping the future of aspiring educators. Your role is one of profound influence, providing a nurturing and empowering space where student teachers can flourish and blossom into their full potential.

This book is a companion, a trusted guide that will walk alongside you as you navigate the intricate path of mentoring. It is designed to equip you with the knowledge, strategies, and insights necessary to excel in your mentoring role and create a meaningful and impactful experience for your mentees.

In Chapter 1: Getting Started: Understanding the Role of a Mentor, we will lay the groundwork for our journey together. We will delve into the importance of mentoring in teacher education and explore the key responsibilities and expectations that come with this noble role. Additionally, we will unravel the art of building a positive mentoring relationship, fostering a connection that is built on trust, respect, and open communication.

Chapter 2: Preparing for Mentoring Success invites you to lay the groundwork for a fruitful and rewarding mentoring experience. We will delve into the significance of setting clear goals and expectations, establishing effective communication channels, and managing your time and workload with intention and purpose. By honing these foundational skills, you will create a solid framework for mentoring success.

As we move forward, Chapter 3: Supporting Student Teacher Development will become our compass, guiding us towards the heart of mentoring. Here, we will explore the art of observing and providing constructive feedback, creating co-planning and co-teaching opportunities, and nurturing reflective practice and self-evaluation. By offering tailored support and guidance, you will empower your student teachers to grow and evolve as educators.

Yet, we must also acknowledge that our path may encounter challenges and obstacles. In Chapter 4: Addressing Challenges and Overcoming Obstacles, we will navigate these trials together. We will uncover strategies for striking the delicate balance between support and independence, mastering the art of managing difficult conversations, and proactively addressing the unique challenges that arise within the classroom. Through resilience and unwavering dedication, we will triumph over adversity.

The journey continues in Chapter 5: Fostering Inclusion and Culturally Responsive Mentoring, where we celebrate the beauty of diversity and inclusivity. Here, we will explore the significance of embracing diversity in the classroom, promoting equity and inclusion, and recognizing and addressing bias. By fostering an environment of cultural responsiveness, we will create transformative educational experiences for all.

In Chapter 6: Ethical Considerations and Professionalism in Mentoring, we embark on a voyage of integrity and professionalism. We will explore the importance of maintaining confidentiality and respecting boundaries, ensuring fairness and equity, and nurturing our own professional growth. By upholding the highest ethical standards, we become beacons of inspiration and guidance.

Chapter 7: Navigating the Assessment and Evaluation Process will be our compass as we navigate the intricate landscape of evaluating student teacher growth and learning. We will discover the power of providing meaningful feedback and support, and the art of comprehensive documentation and reporting. Through these processes, we will ensure accurate assessments and contribute to the growth of our mentees.

In Chapter 8: Self-Care and Personal Well-being for Mentors, we acknowledge the importance of nurturing ourselves as mentors. We will explore strategies for managing stress and avoiding burnout, building a support network of colleagues and peers, and celebrating the successes and achievements of our mentoring journey. By prioritizing our well-being, we strengthen our ability to uplift and inspire others.

As our journey comes to a close, the Conclusion: Reflecting on the Mentoring Journey invites us to pause and reflect on the transformative experiences we have encountered. We will celebrate the growth witnessed, the lessons learned, and the future possibilities that lie ahead. Together, we will honor the immense privilege and responsibility of mentoring, forever transformed by the profound connections we have forged.

So, dear reader, I invite you to immerse yourself in this book, to embrace the wisdom and guidance it offers, and to embark on this mentoring adventure with an open heart and an unwavering commitment to making a difference. May your journey be filled with joy, discovery, and countless moments of profound transformation.

Welcome to the mentoring journey, where together, we shape the future of education.

Warmest regards,

Cheryl

Chapter 1:

Getting Started - Understanding the Role of a Mentor

I vividly remember the first time I stepped into the role of teacher mentor. I had been assigned a bright and eager student teacher, ready to embark on their journey in the world of education. It was a moment of profound responsibility and an opportunity to make a difference in someone's life.

I quickly realized that being a mentor was not just about providing guidance and knowledge; it was about fostering a relationship built on trust, support, and shared learning. I understood that my role was not to simply instruct but to inspire, motivate, and empower my mentee.

In our initial meetings, I took the time to listen attentively to my mentee's aspirations, concerns, and goals. I wanted to understand their unique perspective and tailor my support accordingly. We discussed the expectations and boundaries, ensuring a clear understanding of our roles and responsibilities.

As our mentoring journey progressed, I found myself not only imparting my wisdom but also learning valuable lessons from my mentee. We engaged in meaningful conversations, reflecting on the challenges, triumphs, and growth that occurred along the way. We laughed together, shared stories, and even shed tears during difficult moments. Through it all, our bond grew stronger, and a sense of mutual trust and respect developed.

I realized that being a mentor meant being a constant source of encouragement and a sounding board for ideas. It meant providing constructive feedback that pushed my mentee to strive for excellence while nurturing their self-confidence. It meant creating a safe space for them to ask questions, express doubts, and seek guidance.

Being a mentor is a privilege that comes with the responsibility to shape the future of education. It requires patience, empathy, and a genuine passion for helping others succeed. It is about being a lifelong learner, continuously adapting and growing alongside our mentees.

As I reflect on my journey as a mentor, I am grateful for the transformative experiences we shared, the milestones we celebrated, and the impact we made in each other's lives. It is through understanding the role of a mentor, embracing it wholeheartedly, and building a strong foundation of trust and support that we can truly make a difference in the lives of student teachers and the future of education.

1.1 The Importance of Mentoring in Teacher Education

MENTORING PLAYS A CRUCIAL role in teacher education, shaping the development and success of aspiring educators. It is a dynamic and supportive process that goes beyond traditional instruction, offering invaluable guidance, support, and opportunities for growth. Here we will explore the importance of mentoring in teacher education, highlighting its impact on the professional development and overall preparedness of future teachers.

First and foremost, mentoring provides a bridge between theory and practice, helping student teachers translate their knowledge into effective classroom instruction. While teacher education programs equip students with pedagogical theories and teaching strategies, the practical application of these concepts can be challenging. Mentors serve as experienced guides, offering insights, modeling effective teaching practices, and providing feedback on lesson implementation. Through observation and collaborative planning, mentors help student teachers connect the dots between theory and practice, ensuring they develop a repertoire of teaching skills that can be effectively applied in diverse classroom settings.

Furthermore, mentoring fosters the development of reflective practitioners. The guidance and support provided by mentors encourage student teachers to critically examine their teaching methods, reflect on their experiences, and make adjustments to enhance their instructional practices. Mentors facilitate conversations that promote self-reflection, helping student teachers identify their strengths and areas for improvement. By engaging in reflective dialogue, student teachers gain a deeper understanding of their teaching approach, allowing them to refine their instructional strategies and adapt to the needs of their students. This reflective practice not only improves the quality of their teaching but also cultivates a lifelong commitment to professional growth and continuous improvement.

Mentoring also offers emotional support and encouragement during the demanding journey of becoming a teacher. Student teachers often face challenges such as classroom management issues, curriculum planning dilemmas, and the pressure of meeting students' diverse needs. Mentors provide a safe and supportive environment where student teachers can openly discuss their concerns, seek advice, and receive validation for their efforts. The empathetic guidance of mentors helps student teachers build resilience and confidence, empowering them to overcome obstacles and persist in their pursuit of becoming effective educators.

In addition to these benefits, mentoring facilitates the transfer of practical wisdom and professional values from experienced teachers to future generations. Mentors, drawing on their own experiences and expertise, impart valuable insights on classroom management, instructional strategies, and navigating the complexities of the education system. They model professionalism, ethics, and a commitment to lifelong learning, instilling these essential qualities in their mentees. Through the mentor-mentee relationship, student teachers internalize the values of the profession and develop their own professional identity, ensuring they enter the field equipped with a strong foundation and a deep understanding of their role as educators.

1.2 Key Responsibilities and Expectations of a Mentor

MENTORS PLAY A PIVOTAL role in shaping the professional growth and development of aspiring teachers. As experienced educators, mentors take on the important task of guiding and supporting novice teachers, helping them navigate the complexities of the profession and fostering their success.

One of the primary responsibilities of a mentor is to provide guidance and support to their mentees. Mentors serve as a source of knowledge and expertise, sharing their experiences, insights, and practical wisdom. They offer advice on instructional strategies, classroom management techniques, and curriculum design, helping mentees develop the necessary skills and knowledge to excel in their teaching practice. Moreover, mentors assist mentees in understanding and navigating the administrative and bureaucratic aspects of the education system, such as school policies, assessments, and professional development opportunities.

Effective communication is another vital responsibility of a mentor. Mentors must establish open and honest lines of communication with their mentees, creating a safe space for dialogue, reflection, and feedback. They actively listen to their mentees, valuing their perspectives and concerns, and provide constructive feedback that promotes growth and improvement. By engaging in regular and meaningful conversations, mentors encourage mentees to reflect on their teaching practices, identify areas for development, and set goals for their professional growth. Clear and effective communication lays the foundation for a strong mentor-mentee relationship and fosters a collaborative and supportive learning environment.

Building a trusting and supportive relationship is an essential aspect of effective mentoring. Mentors must create an environment where mentees feel comfortable seeking guidance, sharing their challenges, and expressing their thoughts and feelings openly. They demonstrate empathy, patience, and understanding, acknowledging the unique journey of each mentee and tailoring their support to address individual needs. By establishing a sense of trust and rapport, mentors empower mentees to take risks, embrace new teaching strategies, and develop their own teaching style.

Another key responsibility of a mentor is to model professionalism and ethical behavior. Mentors should exemplify the qualities of an effective educator, including integrity, dedication, and a commitment to lifelong learning. They demonstrate professionalism by being punctual, prepared, and organized in their mentorship meetings and interactions. They also model ethical behavior by maintaining confidentiality, respecting boundaries, and upholding the principles of fairness and equity. By serving as role models, mentors inspire and motivate mentees to embody these qualities and contribute positively to the teaching profession.

Lastly, a mentor must possess a genuine passion for teaching and a strong belief in the potential of every student. They should be committed to fostering an inclusive and equitable learning environment, valuing and celebrating diversity in the classroom. Mentors encourage mentees to embrace culturally responsive teaching practices and promote equity and social justice. By instilling these values in their mentees, mentors contribute to the creation of a more inclusive and empowering educational system.

1.3 Building a Positive Mentoring Relationship

THE MENTORING RELATIONSHIP between an experienced educator and a novice teacher is of paramount importance. This relationship serves as the foundation for professional growth, support, and guidance. In this essay, we will explore the significance of building a positive mentoring relationship, emphasizing the key elements and strategies that contribute to its success.

A positive mentoring relationship is characterized by trust, respect, and open communication. It is a partnership built on mutual understanding and shared goals, where both the mentor and mentee actively contribute to the growth and development of the novice teacher. To establish such a relationship, it is crucial for mentors to create a welcoming and non-judgmental environment that encourages mentees to feel comfortable and confident in seeking guidance and sharing their thoughts and experiences.

One key element of building a positive mentoring relationship is active listening. Mentors must genuinely listen to their mentees, demonstrating attentiveness and empathy. They should create opportunities for mentees to express their concerns, aspirations, and challenges, allowing them to feel heard and understood. By actively listening, mentors gain valuable insights into the mentee's needs, strengths, and areas for growth, which in turn informs the support and guidance they provide.

Effective communication is also paramount in fostering a positive mentoring relationship. Mentors should strive for clear and open communication, ensuring that expectations, goals, and feedback are conveyed in a respectful and constructive manner. Regular and meaningful conversations between the mentor and mentee are essential for addressing concerns, reflecting on teaching practices, and setting goals. By engaging in dialogue, both parties can exchange ideas, share experiences, and collaborate on solutions to challenges.

Trust and respect are fundamental components of a positive mentoring relationship. Mentors must create a safe and supportive space where mentees feel comfortable expressing their vulnerabilities and seeking guidance. Building trust involves maintaining confidentiality, honoring commitments, and demonstrating integrity. Additionally, mentors should respect the unique perspectives and experiences that mentees bring to the table, valuing their contributions and treating them as equal partners in the mentoring process.

Collaboration is another vital aspect of building a positive mentoring relationship. Mentors and mentees should work together to set goals, develop action plans, and engage in co-planning and co-teaching experiences. Collaborative activities foster a sense of shared ownership and allow mentees to learn from the expertise of their mentor. By engaging in collaborative practices, mentees also gain confidence and develop their own teaching style.

Flexibility and adaptability are essential when building a positive mentoring relationship. Mentors should recognize that every mentee is unique, with different strengths, needs, and learning styles. Therefore, mentors must be responsive to these individual differences, tailoring their support and guidance accordingly. They should adapt their mentoring strategies to meet the specific needs of each mentee, while also providing opportunities for mentees to explore their own interests and areas of growth.

Chapter 2:

Preparing for Mentoring Success

One year, after several years of mentoring student teachers in my classroom, I was assigned the role of mentoring a cohort of student teachers around my district. I was thrilled to be visiting multiple schools and working with educators who willingly took the student teachers into their classrooms.

To prepare, I immersed myself in research, attended workshops, and sought advice from other experienced mentors. I wanted to understand the key ingredients for mentoring success and how I could create a supportive and enriching environment for my mentees.

One piece of advice that resonated deeply with me was the importance of setting clear goals and expectations from the outset. I knew that establishing a shared vision and a common understanding of what we wanted to achieve would lay the foundation for a productive and meaningful mentoring relationship.

With this in mind, I arranged an introductory meeting with each of my mentees. We sat down in a cozy corner of each school's staff room, sipped cups of tea, and delved into heartfelt conversations. I wanted to get to know them as individuals and understand their aspirations, strengths, and areas for growth.

During these conversations, we discussed their goals for the mentorship program, what they hoped to achieve, and any specific areas they wanted to focus on. I also shared my own expectations as a mentor, expressing my commitment to their professional development and my belief in their potential to excel.

Together, we crafted a personalized plan that outlined the milestones, strategies, and resources we would utilize throughout our mentoring journey. This plan served as a roadmap, guiding our discussions, observations, and reflections. It provided a sense of structure and direction while allowing for flexibility and individualized support.

Throughout the mentoring process, I made sure to regularly revisit our goals and adjust them as needed. We celebrated achievements, big and small, and used setbacks as opportunities for growth and learning. I provided constructive feedback, highlighting their strengths and offering suggestions for improvement. Most importantly, I created a safe space where they felt comfortable sharing their challenges, seeking guidance, and engaging in reflective conversations.

Preparing for mentoring success also meant recognizing that every mentee is unique and brings their own set of experiences, perspectives, and learning styles. I made a conscious effort to adapt my mentoring approach to meet their individual needs, providing differentiated support and guidance tailored to their specific goals and aspirations.

No matter how many student teachers I've mentored, I recognize that preparing for mentoring success is an ongoing process that requires continuous reflection, refinement, and growth. It is a journey of shared learning, mutual respect, and unwavering commitment.

2.1 Setting Clear Goals and Expectations

SETTING CLEAR GOALS and expectations is a crucial aspect that lays the foundation for a successful mentoring relationship. It provides a roadmap for both the mentor and mentee, guiding their efforts and focusing their energies towards specific objectives.

One of the primary reasons for setting clear goals and expectations is to ensure alignment and clarity between the mentor and mentee. By establishing a shared understanding of what needs to be achieved, both parties can work collaboratively towards a common purpose. Clear goals provide a sense of direction and purpose, enabling the mentor and mentee to channel their efforts effectively and make meaningful progress.

When goals are clearly defined, it becomes easier to monitor and evaluate progress. Both the mentor and mentee can track their achievements, identify areas for improvement, and celebrate milestones along the way. Clear goals also facilitate meaningful feedback and assessment, as they provide a measurable framework against which performance can be evaluated. This feedback loop supports the mentee's growth and development by providing specific areas of focus and opportunities for refinement.

Setting clear goals and expectations also helps in establishing a sense of accountability. Both the mentor and mentee have a shared responsibility to work towards the identified goals and meet the set expectations. This accountability fosters a sense of commitment and dedication to the mentoring process. It also promotes a sense of ownership, empowering the mentee to take charge of their own professional growth and actively engage in the mentoring relationship.

To set clear goals and expectations, it is essential to engage in collaborative discussion. This dialogue allows both parties to express their perspectives, identify strengths and areas for growth, and articulate their aspirations. The mentor, drawing on their experience and expertise, can provide guidance and support in setting realistic and attainable goals. The mentee, on the other hand, can actively contribute their insights, reflecting their personal needs and aspirations.

To ensure that goals and expectations are clear and measurable, they should be specific, achievable, relevant, and time-bound. Specific goals outline the desired outcomes in detail, leaving no room for ambiguity. Achievable goals are realistic and within the mentee's reach, considering their current level of development and available resources. Relevant goals are aligned with the mentee's professional growth and development needs. Finally, time-bound goals are accompanied by a timeline or deadline, providing a sense of urgency and motivation.

Regular communication and ongoing reflection are key components of setting and adjusting goals and expectations. The mentor and mentee should engage in frequent discussions to review progress, provide feedback, and make necessary adjustments. This reflective process allows for the identification of emerging needs and the refinement of goals to ensure they remain relevant and challenging.

Clear goals provide a roadmap for growth, facilitate accountability, and enable progress monitoring. By engaging in collaborative discussions, using specific and measurable criteria, and promoting ongoing reflection, mentors and mentees can establish a solid foundation for achieving success in the mentoring journey.

2.2 Establishing Effective Communication Channels

EFFECTIVE COMMUNICATION is the cornerstone of any successful relationship, and this holds true for the mentor-mentee dynamic as well. In the context of mentoring, establishing effective communication channels is vital for building trust, fostering understanding, and promoting a positive and productive relationship.

Effective communication is essential in mentoring because it allows for the exchange of information, ideas, and feedback between the mentor and mentee. It enables them to share insights, discuss challenges, and seek guidance in a collaborative and supportive manner. By establishing effective communication channels, mentors and mentees can build a strong foundation of mutual respect, trust, and understanding, which forms the basis for a meaningful and impactful mentoring relationship.

One of the key aspects of establishing effective communication channels is creating a safe and non-judgmental space for open dialogue. Both the mentor and mentee should feel comfortable expressing their thoughts, concerns, and aspirations without fear of criticism or judgment. This safe space encourages transparency and authenticity, allowing for genuine and meaningful conversations that lead to growth and development.

Regular and consistent communication is another vital component of effective mentoring. By establishing a predictable communication schedule, such as weekly or bi-weekly meetings, mentors and mentees can ensure that they stay connected and engaged throughout the mentoring process. This regular interaction provides opportunities to discuss progress, share insights, address challenges, and provide guidance and support.

Choosing the right communication channels is crucial for effective communication in mentoring. Depending on individual preferences and logistical considerations, mentors and mentees can utilize various mediums such as face-to-face meetings, phone calls, emails, video conferencing, or even online platforms. It is important to select channels that facilitate clear and timely communication, taking into account factors such as accessibility, convenience, and confidentiality.

Active listening is a fundamental skill that mentors should cultivate to establish effective communication channels. Actively listening involves not only hearing what the mentee is saying but also showing genuine interest and empathy. Mentors should create an environment where mentees feel heard, valued, and understood. This active listening promotes trust, encourages mentees to open up, and allows for more meaningful and productive conversations.

Clear and concise communication is also essential in mentoring. Both mentors and mentees should strive to articulate their thoughts, questions, and feedback in a clear and understandable manner. Using simple and concise language helps avoid misinterpretation or confusion, ensuring that the intended message is accurately conveyed. Additionally, mentors can provide constructive feedback using specific examples and actionable suggestions to guide the mentee's growth and development.

Regular reflection and feedback are integral to maintaining effective communication channels in mentoring. Mentors and mentees should take time to reflect on their interactions, assess the effectiveness of their communication strategies, and provide feedback to one another. This reflective process helps identify areas of improvement, reinforces positive communication patterns, and enhances the overall quality of the mentoring relationship.

By creating a safe and non-judgmental space, maintaining regular and consistent communication, practicing active listening, and promoting clear and concise communication, mentors and mentees can foster understanding, build trust, and facilitate meaningful growth and development. Effective communication is the key to unlocking the full potential of mentoring and maximizing its impact on the mentee's professional journey.

2.3 Managing Time and Workload

TIME MANAGEMENT AND workload organization are crucial skills for mentors in effectively supporting their mentees. In the context of mentoring, mentors play a pivotal role in guiding and supporting the mentee's professional growth. However, mentors often have their own professional responsibilities and commitments, making it essential to effectively manage their time and workload to provide the necessary support.

One of the primary challenges mentors face is balancing their mentoring responsibilities with their existing workload. Mentors often have teaching, administrative, and other professional obligations that require their time and attention. It is important for mentors to recognize the significance of their mentoring role and allocate sufficient time and resources to fulfill their commitments to their mentees.

Effective time management is essential in mentoring as it allows mentors to prioritize their tasks and responsibilities. Mentors can start by assessing their existing workload and identifying areas where they can delegate, automate, or streamline their responsibilities. This evaluation helps mentors identify time-consuming tasks that can be optimized to free up more time for mentoring activities.

Creating a structured schedule is a helpful strategy for managing time and workload. Mentors can allocate specific time slots for mentoring-related activities, such as meetings, observations, and feedback sessions. By setting aside dedicated time for these tasks, mentors can ensure they have sufficient time to provide meaningful support to their mentees without feeling overwhelmed by competing demands.

Another aspect of managing time and workload is setting realistic expectations and boundaries. Mentors should have open and honest conversations with their mentees about their availability and the extent of support they can provide. By clearly communicating their limitations and establishing boundaries, mentors can ensure that mentees have realistic expectations and are aware of any time constraints or other factors that may affect the mentor's availability.

Delegating tasks and responsibilities is an effective strategy to manage time and workload. Where possible, mentors should identify tasks that can be delegated to others, such as administrative tasks or paperwork, to free up time for mentoring activities. This may involve collaborating with colleagues, support staff, or mentee's cooperating teachers to share responsibilities and ensure that the workload is distributed more evenly.

Utilizing technology and organizational tools can also enhance time management and workload organization. Mentors can leverage digital tools, such as scheduling apps, task management software, or shared online platforms, to streamline communication, track progress, and manage mentoring-related tasks efficiently. These tools can help mentors stay organized, prioritize tasks, and ensure that important deadlines or commitments are not overlooked.

Lastly, mentors should practice self-care and prioritize their well-being. Effective time management requires balancing professional responsibilities with personal needs. Mentors should schedule time for relaxation, exercise, and self-reflection to avoid burnout and maintain their own well-being. By taking care of themselves, mentors can approach their mentoring responsibilities with renewed energy and enthusiasm.

Chapter 3:

Supporting Student Teacher Development

My mentee, Sarah, greeted me with a warm smile and a hint of apprehension in her eyes. She had just started her placement and was eager to learn and make a positive impact on her students. As her mentor, it was my responsibility to guide and empower her throughout this transformative experience.

One of the key aspects of supporting Sarah's development was observing her instruction and providing constructive feedback. I would sit at the back of the classroom, discreetly taking notes on her teaching techniques, interactions with students, and overall classroom management. After each observation, we would meet to discuss her strengths, areas for improvement, and strategies for growth.

During our feedback sessions, I made sure to provide specific examples and actionable suggestions. I focused on highlighting Sarah's successes and the positive impact she was making on her students. At the same time, I gently addressed areas where she could refine her instructional strategies or implement alternative approaches. It was important for her to feel supported and encouraged in her journey of continuous improvement.

To further support Sarah's development, we also engaged in co-planning and co-teaching opportunities. We would collaboratively design lesson plans, incorporating differentiated instruction, active learning strategies, and assessment practices. By working side by side, I was able to model effective teaching techniques and help her navigate the intricacies of classroom management.

These co-teaching experiences not only provided Sarah with hands-on guidance and support but also allowed her to gradually take on more responsibility. As her confidence grew, I gradually stepped back, allowing her to independently lead lessons while offering support from the sidelines.

Nurturing reflective practice and self-evaluation was another essential aspect of supporting Sarah's development. We engaged in regular reflective conversations, encouraging her to analyze her teaching practices, evaluate student outcomes, and identify areas for further growth. Through these discussions, Sarah learned to critically examine her lessons, make adjustments, and set goals for her professional development.

Throughout our mentoring journey, I made it a priority to create a supportive and trusting relationship with Sarah. We had open and honest conversations, sharing our triumphs, challenges, and even moments of self-doubt. I encouraged her to embrace her unique teaching style, celebrate her successes, and learn from setbacks.

Witnessing Sarah's growth as an educator was immensely rewarding. From a nervous student teacher to a confident and capable educator, she blossomed in her ability to create engaging lessons, foster a positive classroom culture, and meet the diverse needs of her students.

3.1 Observing and Providing Constructive Feedback

OBSERVATION AND FEEDBACK are vital components of the mentoring process, allowing mentors to assess the progress of their mentees and provide valuable guidance for growth and improvement.

Observation serves as a powerful tool for mentors to gain insights into their mentees' teaching practices, classroom dynamics, and student interactions. Through observation, mentors can identify strengths and areas for development, observe instructional strategies in action, and assess the overall effectiveness of the mentee's teaching approach. It provides an opportunity to gather evidence, analyze teaching practices, and make informed decisions to guide the mentee's professional growth.

To conduct effective observations, mentors should establish a purpose and focus for each observation session. They should communicate the observation goals with the mentee beforehand, ensuring both parties are clear about what aspects of teaching and learning will be observed and evaluated. This clarity promotes a collaborative approach to observation, where the mentee actively participates and engages in reflective dialogue.

During the observation, mentors should adopt an objective and non-judgmental stance, focusing on gathering accurate and unbiased information. They should take detailed notes, capturing specific examples of effective practices, areas for improvement, and noteworthy student interactions. These observations should be evidence-based and aligned with the mentee's professional goals and teaching standards.

After the observation, mentors should schedule a feedback session to discuss their observations and provide constructive feedback. Constructive feedback is aimed at helping the mentee identify areas of strength, areas for improvement, and actionable steps for growth. It is important for mentors to create a supportive and non-threatening environment, where the mentee feels comfortable receiving feedback and is encouraged to reflect on their teaching practices.

When delivering feedback, mentors should focus on specific examples and evidence from the observation, providing clear and specific suggestions for improvement. They should balance positive reinforcement with areas of growth, acknowledging the mentee's strengths while highlighting opportunities for enhancement. By framing feedback as a collaborative conversation rather than a critique, mentors can foster a growth mindset and create a safe space for the mentee to ask questions and seek clarification.

Mentors should also encourage self-reflection in the feedback process, prompting the mentee to analyze their own teaching practices and critically assess their impact on student learning. This reflection helps mentees develop a deeper understanding of their teaching approaches, make connections between theory and practice, and identify strategies for continuous improvement.

3.2 Co-planning and Co-teaching Opportunities

CO-PLANNING AND CO-teaching are collaborative practices that promote effective partnerships between mentors and mentees, fostering professional growth and enhancing student learning outcomes.

Co-planning involves mentors and mentees working together to design and develop lesson plans, units, and instructional strategies. It is a collaborative process where both parties contribute their expertise, knowledge, and perspectives to create meaningful learning experiences for students. Co-planning allows for the sharing of ideas, brainstorming, and aligning instructional goals and objectives.

During the co-planning process, mentors can guide mentees in understanding curriculum requirements, selecting appropriate instructional materials, and incorporating effective pedagogical strategies. Mentees can also contribute their fresh perspectives, creativity, and knowledge of their students' needs and interests. This collaborative effort ensures that lessons are well-designed, engaging, and tailored to meet the diverse needs of the students.

Co-planning provides an opportunity for mentors to model effective instructional practices and demonstrate how to integrate best practices into lesson design. Through this process, mentees can observe and learn from their mentors' expertise, gaining insights into effective teaching strategies, differentiation techniques, and assessment methods. Co-planning allows for shared decision-making, fostering a sense of ownership and investment in the teaching and learning process.

Co-teaching takes the collaboration a step further by involving mentors and mentees in joint instructional delivery. In a co-teaching setting, mentors and mentees share responsibility for planning, delivering, and assessing instruction. This approach provides mentees with opportunities to observe their mentors in action, learn new instructional techniques, and receive immediate feedback on their teaching practices.

Co-teaching can take various forms, such as station teaching, parallel teaching, alternative teaching, or team teaching. Each approach allows for the mentee to actively participate in delivering instruction, gradually assuming more responsibility as their confidence and skills develop. Co-teaching allows for the mentee to benefit from the expertise of their mentor while gaining practical experience in a supported environment.

Flexibility and open-mindedness are key to successful co-planning and co-teaching. Mentors should be receptive to new ideas and perspectives from their mentees, while mentees should be willing to learn from their mentors' expertise and experience. Both parties should embrace a growth mindset, seeing co-planning and co-teaching as opportunities for continuous learning and improvement.

These practices foster a supportive and dynamic learning environment, benefiting both the mentee's professional growth and the overall success of student learning. By embracing co-planning and co-teaching, mentors and mentees can create meaningful and impactful learning experiences that promote student achievement and teacher effectiveness.

3.3 Nurturing Reflective Practice and Self-evaluation

PROFESSIONAL GROWTH and development go hand in hand with reflective practice and self-evaluation. As mentors, it is our responsibility to support and nurture this process in our mentees, as it plays a pivotal role in their continuous improvement as educators.

Reflective practice involves critically examining one's teaching experiences, analyzing the effectiveness of instructional strategies, and reflecting on the impact on student learning. It is a deliberate and intentional process that allows mentees to gain deeper insights into their teaching practices, strengths, areas for growth, and the overall effectiveness of their instruction. Through reflection, mentees can make informed decisions about instructional adjustments and improvements, ultimately enhancing their teaching practice.

One of the essential aspects of nurturing reflective practice is creating a supportive and non-judgmental environment where mentees feel safe to openly reflect on their experiences. Mentors should encourage mentees to engage in self-reflection by asking probing questions, such as "What worked well in this lesson?", "What challenges did you encounter?", and "How did the students respond to the instruction?".

Mentors can guide mentees through the process of reflection by modeling reflective practices themselves. Sharing personal anecdotes, successes, and challenges from their own teaching experiences can help mentees see the value and importance of reflection in professional growth. Mentors can also provide prompts or journaling activities to help mentees structure their reflections and focus on specific areas of interest or concern.

Self-evaluation is closely linked to reflective practice and involves assessing one's teaching performance against established standards or goals. It requires mentees to critically analyze their instructional practices, student outcomes, and their own professional growth. Self-evaluation empowers mentees to take ownership of their development, as they become active participants in the assessment and improvement of their teaching effectiveness.

Regular check-ins and feedback sessions are essential for fostering self-evaluation. Mentors should provide constructive feedback that highlights both strengths and areas for improvement, encouraging mentees to reflect on their practice and identify strategies for growth. Mentors can also facilitate collaborative discussions where mentees can share their self-evaluation findings and insights with their peers, promoting a culture of mutual learning and support.

Additionally, mentors can introduce mentees to various self-assessment tools and resources that can aid in their self-evaluation process. These may include rubrics, checklists, video recordings of their teaching, or self-reflection templates. These tools can provide mentees with a structured framework for analyzing their teaching practices, identifying areas of growth, and planning for future improvements.

The benefits of nurturing reflective practice and self-evaluation are numerous. Mentees who engage in reflective practice become more self-aware, develop a deeper understanding of their teaching, and become proactive in their professional growth. Through self-evaluation, mentees can identify their strengths and areas for improvement, set goals, and take deliberate steps towards enhancing their teaching effectiveness.

Chapter 4:

Addressing Challenges and Overcoming Obstacles

Throughout my years as a mentor, one particular memory from my time as a faculty advisor stands out—the time when my mentee, Alex, faced a major obstacle that seemed insurmountable. It was during his student teaching placement, and he had encountered a challenging classroom dynamic that tested his patience, resilience, and ability to maintain a positive learning environment.

Alex had been assigned to a middle school classroom with a diverse group of students, each with their own unique needs and behaviors. While he had carefully prepared his lessons and implemented various classroom management strategies, he found himself struggling to engage certain students and maintain order in the classroom.

One day, I received a distressed message from Alex, expressing his frustration and seeking guidance. We scheduled a meeting to discuss the challenges he was facing. As we sat down together, I could see the weariness in his eyes, but I also sensed his determination to overcome this hurdle.

During our conversation, Alex shared the specific behaviors he was encountering in the classroom—disruptive outbursts, lack of participation, and resistance to authority. Together, we analyzed the underlying causes of these behaviors and brainstormed strategies to address them effectively.

We decided to take a collaborative approach, involving both Alex and the students in finding solutions. We held a class meeting where students were given the opportunity to express their concerns and suggest ways to improve the classroom environment. It was important for Alex to empower the students and create a sense of ownership and responsibility within the classroom community.

Through open and honest dialogue, we identified underlying issues such as lack of motivation, social dynamics, and individual needs that were not being met. Armed with this understanding, we developed a plan to address each challenge strategically.

Alex began implementing small changes, such as incorporating more student choice in assignments, providing additional support to struggling students, and fostering a sense of inclusivity and respect. He also implemented a system of rewards and recognition to acknowledge positive behaviors and achievements.

The road ahead was not without its bumps, but Alex remained committed to the process. We met regularly to assess progress, make adjustments, and provide ongoing support. Alex sought feedback from colleagues, attended professional development workshops, and engaged in self-reflection to refine his teaching strategies.

Over time, we began to witness a transformation within the classroom. The disruptive behaviors decreased, and students started to actively participate, demonstrate increased engagement, and show respect towards one another. The positive changes in the classroom dynamic were a testament to Alex's dedication, perseverance, and his willingness to adapt and learn from the challenges he faced.

Alex's experience taught me the value of perseverance and the profound impact a mentor can have in supporting a mentee through challenging times. As mentors, it is our responsibility to provide guidance, encouragement, and a safe space for reflection, empowering student teachers to face obstacles head-on and emerge as resilient professionals.

4.1 Balancing Support and Independence

AS MENTORS, ONE OF our fundamental roles is to strike a delicate balance between providing support and fostering independence in our mentees. It is crucial to create an environment where mentees feel supported and guided, while also encouraging their autonomy and self-directed growth.

Support is essential for mentees, especially when they are navigating the complexities of teaching and gaining confidence in their abilities. Mentors must be readily available to lend a helping hand, offer guidance, and provide the necessary resources to support mentees' professional growth. This support can come in various forms, such as sharing instructional strategies, suggesting relevant literature, or discussing classroom management techniques.

However, it is equally important to encourage mentees to develop their own voice and teaching style. Mentors should promote mentees' autonomy and encourage them to take ownership of their teaching practice. Allowing mentees to make decisions, take risks, and learn from their experiences fosters a sense of independence and self-efficacy. Mentees should feel empowered to experiment with instructional approaches, adapt strategies to meet the needs of their students, and develop their unique teaching identity.

To strike a balance between support and independence, mentors can gradually shift from a more directive approach to a facilitative one. Initially, mentors may provide explicit guidance and demonstrate effective teaching practices. As mentees gain confidence and experience, mentors can gradually transition into a supportive role, offering guidance through questioning, providing opportunities for mentees to reflect on their practice, and encouraging critical thinking.

Building trust and open communication is crucial in achieving a balance between support and independence. Mentees should feel comfortable seeking guidance and sharing their challenges and successes with their mentors. Mentors should actively listen to mentees' concerns, validate their experiences, and provide constructive feedback that encourages independent thinking and decision-making. Regular check-ins and reflective discussions can help mentors gauge the level of support needed by their mentees at different stages of their development.

It is essential for mentors to be mindful of the individual needs and readiness of each mentee. Some mentees may require more support initially, while others may be eager to take on greater independence from the start. Mentors should adapt their approach accordingly and differentiate their support to meet the unique needs of each student teacher.

By striking a balance between support and independence, mentors enable mentees to develop their confidence, competence, and leadership skills. Mentees who feel supported yet empowered to make decisions become more invested in their professional growth. They become resilient, adaptable, and reflective practitioners who are capable of navigating the challenges of the teaching profession.

4.2 Managing Difficult Conversations

IN ANY MENTORING RELATIONSHIP, there may come a time when difficult conversations need to be addressed. These conversations can arise from various situations, such as addressing performance issues, providing constructive feedback, or discussing sensitive topics. Effectively managing difficult conversations is an essential skill for mentors to ensure a positive and growth-oriented mentoring experience.

One of the key principles in managing difficult conversations is establishing a foundation of trust and mutual respect. Mentees should feel safe and comfortable expressing their thoughts and concerns without fear of judgment or reprisal. As mentors, it is essential to create an open and non-threatening space where mentees can freely communicate their perspectives. Active listening, empathy, and validating mentees' experiences are crucial in building trust and fostering open communication.

Before engaging in a difficult conversation, mentors should take the time to plan and prepare. Clarify the purpose and desired outcome of the conversation, and gather relevant information or evidence to support your points. Consider the timing and setting of the conversation, ensuring privacy and minimizing distractions. Being well-prepared will increase your confidence and enable you to navigate the conversation more effectively.

During the conversation, mentors should strive for clarity and assertiveness while maintaining a respectful and empathetic tone. Start by expressing your observations or concerns using specific examples and focusing on behavior or performance rather than personal traits. Use "I" statements to communicate your perspective and avoid sounding accusatory or judgmental. It is important to listen actively to mentees' responses, asking clarifying questions to ensure a thorough understanding of their point of view.

Emotional intelligence plays a vital role in managing difficult conversations. Mentors should be aware of their own emotions and manage them effectively during the conversation. Remain calm, composed, and non-defensive, even in the face of challenging or emotional responses from mentees. Validate mentees' emotions and demonstrate empathy, showing that you understand and acknowledge their feelings.

When providing feedback or addressing concerns, mentors should strive for a balance between being supportive and challenging. Offer constructive criticism with a focus on specific areas for improvement and suggestions for growth. Frame feedback as an opportunity for learning and development, emphasizing the mentees' strengths and potential. Collaboratively explore possible solutions or strategies to address the identified issues, involving mentees in the problem-solving process.

Active listening and effective questioning techniques are invaluable in managing difficult conversations. Encourage mentees to share their perspectives, actively listen to their viewpoints, and ask probing questions to elicit deeper reflection and understanding. Seek to find common ground and areas of agreement, as this can foster a sense of collaboration and shared responsibility for growth.

It is also important to remember that difficult conversations should not end on a negative note. Aim to conclude the conversation by highlighting areas of progress, reinforcing the mentees' strengths, and expressing confidence in their ability to address the challenges discussed. Offer ongoing support and follow-up, ensuring that mentees feel supported in their growth journey.

Lastly, reflecting on difficult conversations is crucial for mentors' continuous improvement. Take the time to assess your own communication style, strengths, and areas for growth. Consider seeking feedback from mentees to gain insights into their experience of the conversation and your mentoring approach. Reflecting on these conversations can help mentors refine their skills, enhance their communication strategies, and foster stronger mentoring relationships.

4.3 Dealing with Classroom Challenges

WHEN MENTORING STUDENT teachers, classroom challenges are inevitable. These challenges can range from student behavior issues to curriculum implementation struggles, and they require mentors to navigate them effectively to support the growth and development of their mentees.

First and foremost, mentors should encourage open and ongoing communication with their mentees regarding the classroom challenges they encounter. By fostering a safe and non-judgmental space, mentors can create an environment where mentees feel comfortable discussing their concerns and seeking guidance. Regular check-ins and debriefing sessions allow mentors to stay informed about the challenges faced by their mentees and offer timely support.

When addressing classroom challenges, it is crucial for mentors to adopt a problem-solving mindset. Mentors can guide mentees in analyzing the root causes of the challenges and collaboratively develop strategies to address them. Encourage mentees to reflect on their teaching practices, classroom management techniques, and instructional approaches to identify areas for improvement. By engaging mentees in the problem-solving process, mentors empower them to take ownership of their professional growth and development.

One effective approach to dealing with classroom challenges is providing mentees with practical strategies and resources. Mentors can share their own experiences and expertise, offering insights into effective instructional practices, behavior management techniques, and differentiated instruction strategies. Mentors should also encourage mentees to seek out additional resources, such as professional literature, workshops, or peer support networks, to further enhance their teaching repertoire.

Classroom observations allow mentors to identify specific areas for improvement, provide real-time feedback, and offer targeted guidance. By observing classroom dynamics and interactions, mentors can provide tailored support to address the specific challenges mentees encounter.

Dealing with classroom challenges also requires mentors to help mentees develop resilience and problem-solving skills. Encourage mentees to reflect on their experiences, learn from setbacks, and adapt their instructional strategies accordingly. Foster a growth mindset by emphasizing that challenges are opportunities for learning and improvement. By instilling a sense of resilience, mentors empower mentees to overcome obstacles and thrive in their teaching practice.

Lastly, mentors should promote self-care and well-being among their mentees. The demands of teaching can be physically and emotionally draining, especially when faced with classroom challenges. Encourage mentees to prioritize self-care activities, such as exercise, relaxation techniques, and maintaining a healthy work-life balance. By taking care of their well-being, mentees can better cope with challenges and sustain their passion for teaching.

Chapter 5:

Ethical Considerations and Professionalism in Mentoring

In my role as a mentor, I had the privilege of guiding a novice teacher named David through his first year of teaching. As our mentoring relationship developed, it became evident that David was facing some personal challenges outside of the classroom. During one of our mentoring sessions, he opened up and shared some deeply personal information with me.

David expressed his concerns about these challenges affecting his overall well-being and, consequently, his teaching performance. He confided in me, seeking guidance and support in navigating these personal struggles while maintaining his professionalism in the classroom.

Understanding the significance of confidentiality in our mentor-mentee relationship, I assured David that our conversation would remain strictly confidential. I emphasized that the information he shared would be kept private and not disclosed to anyone without his explicit consent. This assurance allowed him to speak openly and honestly, knowing that he could trust me as his mentor.

We discussed strategies to help David manage his personal challenges while maintaining his focus and effectiveness as a teacher. Together, we explored self-care practices, stress management techniques, and resources available to support him outside of the school setting. I encouraged him to seek professional help if needed, assuring him that it was a sign of strength to reach out for assistance.

Throughout the mentoring process, I consistently respected David's privacy and confidentiality. Our discussions remained confidential, and I ensured that any notes or records related to our conversations were securely stored and only accessible by me.

By maintaining confidentiality, I created a safe space for David to share his concerns, seek advice, and receive the support he needed. This allowed us to address his personal challenges while also focusing on his professional growth and development as a teacher.

As the school year progressed, David gradually overcame his personal struggles and found a renewed sense of purpose and confidence in his teaching. Our commitment to confidentiality and trust strengthened our mentoring relationship, enabling David to flourish both personally and professionally.

5.1 Maintaining Confidentiality and Respecting Boundaries

CONFIDENTIALITY AND respecting boundaries are crucial aspects of the mentoring relationship. As mentors, we hold a position of trust and responsibility, and it is essential that we uphold the privacy and boundaries of our mentees.

Confidentiality is the cornerstone of a trusting mentoring relationship. When student teachers share their challenges, concerns, and personal experiences, it is our duty to keep this information confidential unless there is a legal or ethical obligation to disclose it. Respecting confidentiality demonstrates our commitment to the well-being and trust of our mentees. It allows student teachers to feel safe to discuss sensitive matters, ask questions, and seek guidance without the fear of their information being shared inappropriately.

To maintain confidentiality, mentors must clearly communicate the boundaries and expectations around privacy from the beginning of the mentoring relationship. This includes discussing the limits of confidentiality, such as situations where information may need to be shared with school administrators, supervisors, or when there is a potential risk to the safety and well-being of the student teacher or others. Establishing these boundaries early on helps to build trust and ensures that both parties are aware of the expectations regarding confidentiality.

Respecting boundaries goes beyond maintaining confidentiality. It involves recognizing and honoring the personal boundaries of our mentees in various aspects of the mentoring relationship. Boundaries can include physical, emotional, and professional limits. Mentors should be mindful of their interactions with student teachers and ensure that they are respectful, professional, and considerate at all times.

One way to respect boundaries is by actively listening to our mentees and acknowledging their feelings and perspectives without judgment or imposing our own beliefs. This creates a safe space where student teachers feel comfortable expressing themselves authentically. Additionally, mentors should be mindful of the power dynamics inherent in the mentoring relationship and strive to create a balanced and equitable dynamic. This includes encouraging open dialogue, valuing student teachers' opinions and ideas, and promoting their autonomy and agency in decision-making processes.

Another crucial aspect of respecting boundaries is being aware of and responsive to the individual needs and preferences of our mentees. Different student teachers may have varying comfort levels when it comes to sharing personal information or seeking support. It is important to be sensitive to their boundaries and provide support in a manner that aligns with their preferences. Some student teachers may prefer more frequent check-ins and guidance, while others may require more independent learning and reflection time. By adapting our mentoring approach to meet their needs, we demonstrate our respect for their boundaries and support their professional growth.

5.2 Professional Growth and Continuous Improvement

PROFESSIONAL GROWTH and continuous improvement are vital aspects of the mentoring process for student teachers. As mentors, it is our responsibility to support the development of our mentees and encourage their ongoing growth as educators.

Professional growth refers to the deliberate effort of student teachers to enhance their knowledge, skills, and dispositions as educators. It involves a commitment to lifelong learning, self-reflection, and seeking opportunities for personal and professional development. As mentors, we play an integral role in facilitating and guiding this growth process.

One way to promote professional growth is by helping student teachers set clear and attainable goals. By collaborating with them, we can identify areas in which they would like to improve and develop specific objectives that align with their interests and career aspirations. These goals may encompass pedagogical skills, content knowledge, classroom management strategies, or other aspects of teaching practice.

Additionally, mentors can provide guidance and resources to support student teachers in achieving their goals. This may involve recommending relevant literature, suggesting professional development workshops or conferences, or connecting them with experienced educators who can serve as advisors or role models. By providing access to these resources and opportunities, we empower student teachers to actively engage in their own professional growth.

Continuous improvement, on the other hand, involves an ongoing cycle of reflection, feedback, and refinement of teaching practices. It requires student teachers to critically evaluate their instructional approaches, classroom management strategies, and assessment methods. As mentors, we can guide this process by providing constructive feedback, facilitating reflective discussions, and encouraging student teachers to experiment with new ideas and techniques.

One effective strategy to foster continuous improvement is through regular observations and feedback sessions. By observing our mentees in action, we gain insights into their teaching strengths and areas for improvement. Subsequently, we can provide specific, actionable feedback that focuses on both their successes and areas that need further development. This feedback should be delivered in a supportive and non-judgmental manner, emphasizing growth and learning rather than criticism.

Furthermore, mentors can encourage student teachers to engage in self-reflection as a means of continuous improvement. This can be facilitated through journaling, self-assessment tools, or guided reflection exercises. By encouraging student teachers to analyze their experiences, critically evaluate their teaching practices, and identify areas for growth, we promote a culture of continuous learning and improvement.

Collaboration and sharing best practices are also instrumental in supporting professional growth and continuous improvement. Mentors can facilitate opportunities for student teachers to collaborate with their peers, participate in professional learning communities, or engage in lesson study groups. By creating spaces for sharing ideas, experiences, and strategies, we foster a collaborative learning environment that encourages experimentation and innovation.

Chapter 6:

Navigating the Assessment and Evaluation Process

I vividly remember the day when I sat down with my mentee to discuss her progress and growth as an aspiring educator. We both recognized the significance of this assessment and evaluation process in her journey towards becoming a confident and capable teacher.

As I carefully reviewed her lesson plans, observed her classroom interactions, and analyzed her reflections, I couldn't help but feel a deep sense of pride. It was evident that she had invested countless hours into honing her teaching skills, incorporating feedback, and pushing herself to new heights. Her passion for education radiated through her thoughtful instructional strategies and the meaningful connections she fostered with her students.

However, as a mentor, my role was not only to celebrate her achievements but also to provide constructive feedback that would propel her growth further. With great care and empathy, I highlighted areas where she could refine her instructional techniques, address classroom management challenges, and deepen her understanding of differentiated instruction. Together, we engaged in an open and honest dialogue, sharing insights, exploring strategies, and envisioning her future as an educator.

Navigating the assessment and evaluation process was not about judgment or criticism; rather, it was about fostering a growth-oriented mindset and nurturing a deep commitment to continuous improvement. It was a collaborative effort, grounded in trust and mutual respect. As a mentor, it was my responsibility to create a safe space for her to reflect on her practice, embrace her strengths, and address areas for growth. Through our discussions, she discovered her own potential and found the motivation to push herself even further.

As I witnessed her growth unfold, I felt a deep sense of fulfillment, knowing that I had played a role in shaping her development as an educator. The assessment and evaluation process, though at times challenging, had become a transformative experience, forging a stronger mentor-mentee bond and igniting a passion for lifelong learning.

6.1 Assessing Student Teacher Growth and Learning

ASSESSING THE GROWTH and learning of student teachers is a fundamental aspect of the mentoring process. As mentors, it is crucial for us to evaluate their progress and provide meaningful feedback that supports their professional development.

Assessment serves multiple purposes in the mentoring relationship. First and foremost, it allows mentors to gauge the effectiveness of their guidance and support. By assessing student teacher growth, mentors can determine the impact of their mentoring practices, identify areas of strength, and pinpoint areas that require further attention and development.

Furthermore, assessment provides student teachers with valuable insights into their own progress and areas for improvement. It helps them understand their strengths, recognize areas where they have made significant growth, and identify aspects of their teaching practice that need refinement. This self-awareness is essential for their continued professional growth and development.

To effectively assess student teacher growth and learning, mentors can utilize a range of assessment strategies and tools. These may include formal and informal observations, self-reflection exercises, student feedback, portfolio reviews, and structured assessments such as lesson plans or unit designs. By employing a variety of assessment methods, mentors can gain a comprehensive understanding of the student teacher's progress and provide well-rounded feedback.

When conducting observations, mentors should focus on specific teaching components, such as classroom management, instructional strategies, student engagement, and assessment practices. By using structured observation protocols, mentors can provide targeted feedback on these areas and help student teachers refine their teaching skills.

In addition to formal assessments, mentors should encourage student teachers to engage in self-reflection as a means of assessing their own growth. Reflection exercises, journaling, and self-assessment tools can support this process. These activities prompt student teachers to analyze their teaching practices, reflect on their experiences, and evaluate their progress towards their goals.

Another valuable source of assessment is obtaining feedback from students. Student feedback can provide valuable insights into the impact of the student teacher's instruction and their ability to engage and support student learning. Student feedback allows student teachers to gain a better understanding of their impact on student learning and make adjustments as necessary.

Mentors should provide constructive feedback that highlights areas of growth and suggests strategies for improvement. Feedback should be specific, actionable, and focused on the student teacher's goals and areas of development. Mentors should aim to create a supportive and non-judgmental environment that encourages open dialogue and growth-oriented feedback.

Assessment should not be limited to summative evaluations or end-of-placement assessments. Instead, it should be an ongoing process throughout the mentoring journey. Regular check-ins, feedback sessions, and collaborative discussions provide opportunities for mentors and student teachers to reflect on progress, set new goals, and make adjustments to their practice.

6.2 Providing Meaningful Feedback and

Support

ONE OF THE MOST POWERFUL tools at our disposal when mentoring is the ability to provide meaningful feedback and support. Effective feedback not only helps student teachers understand their strengths and areas for improvement, but it also fosters their professional growth and development.

Meaningful feedback is essential for student teachers to reflect on their teaching practice and make informed adjustments. It helps them understand their progress, identify areas of strength, and recognize opportunities for growth. By providing specific and actionable feedback, mentors can guide student teachers towards enhancing their instructional techniques, classroom management skills, and overall pedagogical approach.

When delivering feedback, mentors should use clear and concise language to ensure that their message is easily understood. They should provide specific examples and observations to illustrate their points and avoid generalizations. By being specific, mentors can highlight both the successes and areas for improvement, allowing student teachers to gain a comprehensive understanding of their teaching practice.

Moreover, feedback should be timely. Providing feedback promptly after observations or teaching experiences allows student teachers to reflect on their performance while the experience is still fresh in their minds. Timely feedback helps them connect their actions to specific outcomes and supports immediate improvement.

In addition to providing feedback on areas of growth, mentors should also acknowledge and reinforce the strengths and successes. Recognizing student teachers' accomplishments boosts confidence and motivation, encouraging them to continue their professional development journey. Balancing constructive feedback with positive reinforcement creates a supportive environment that fosters growth and learning.

To ensure that feedback is meaningful and impactful, mentors should engage in open and honest communication with student teachers. They should create a safe and non-judgmental space where student teachers feel comfortable sharing their concerns, asking questions, and seeking clarification. By establishing a trusting relationship, mentors can provide feedback that is personalized and tailored to the individual needs and goals of the student teacher.

6.3 Documentation and Reporting

DOCUMENTATION AND REPORTING play a vital role in tracking progress, communicating observations, and providing evidence of growth and development when mentoring student teachers. Effective documentation and reporting not only serve as a record-keeping tool but also contribute to the overall assessment and evaluation of student teachers' performance.

Documentation serves as a means to capture important moments and key aspects of student teachers' teaching experiences. It allows mentors to record observations, note significant milestones, and document the implementation of strategies and instructional techniques. By keeping detailed records, mentors can provide objective evidence of the student teacher's growth and progress over time.

Accurate and comprehensive documentation provides a foundation for effective reporting. It enables mentors to provide valuable feedback to student teachers and facilitate meaningful discussions regarding their teaching practice. Documentation allows mentors to refer back to specific instances and examples when discussing strengths, areas for improvement, and progress made by the student teacher.

To ensure effective documentation, mentors should establish a system that captures relevant information in a structured and organized manner. This system may include observation forms, checklists, anecdotal notes, or digital platforms that facilitate easy access and retrieval of information. By having a clear framework for documentation, mentors can ensure consistency and thoroughness in their records.

When documenting observations, mentors should focus on both the observable behaviors and the impact on student learning. They should describe specific teaching strategies used, classroom interactions, and the effectiveness of instructional techniques. It is essential to provide concrete examples, such as student work samples or photographs, to support the documented observations.

Additionally, mentors should maintain open lines of communication with student teachers to gather their input and perspective. Engaging student teachers in the documentation process allows them to reflect on their practice, share insights, and provide self-assessment. By involving student teachers in the documentation process, mentors can create a more comprehensive and accurate picture of their teaching journey.

Reporting is an essential component of the mentoring process, as it provides a formal mechanism for sharing information about the student teacher's progress and growth. Reports should be clear, concise, and objective, focusing on both strengths and areas for improvement. They should highlight the student teacher's achievements, challenges overcome, and future goals.

Chapter 7:

Self-Care and Personal Well-being for Mentors

I vividly remember a time when I was overwhelmed with responsibilities both inside and outside of the mentoring relationship. I was juggling multiple mentees, my own teaching responsibilities, and personal commitments. As a result, I began to feel physically and emotionally drained, finding it increasingly challenging to provide the guidance and support my mentees needed.

One day, during a mentoring session, I shared my struggles with a trusted colleague. She reminded me of the importance of self-care and encouraged me to take time for myself. It was a wake-up call that I needed to prioritize my well-being to be a more effective mentor.

I began incorporating self-care practices into my routine. I made time for activities that brought me joy and relaxation, such as reading, exercising, and spending quality time with loved ones. I also started setting boundaries and saying no when necessary, ensuring I had time to recharge and rejuvenate.

As I started prioritizing my own well-being, I noticed a significant positive shift in my mentoring relationships. I had more energy and enthusiasm to support my mentees. I became a better listener, providing them with undivided attention during our sessions. I was able to offer valuable insights and guidance because I was in a healthier mental and emotional state.

Taking care of myself not only benefited my own well-being but also had a direct impact on the mentees I supported. They witnessed the positive changes in my approach, and it encouraged them to prioritize their own self-care as well. We engaged in conversations about work-life balance, stress management, and the importance of setting boundaries.

By prioritizing self-care and personal well-being, I became a more resilient and effective mentor. I realized that taking care of myself was not a selfish act but a necessary one for me to continue supporting and guiding my mentees effectively.

7.1 Managing Stress and Burnout

TEACHING IS A REWARDING and fulfilling profession, but it can also be demanding and stressful. The pressures of lesson planning, classroom management, meeting deadlines, and juggling multiple responsibilities can take a toll on teachers, including mentors working with student teachers.

Stress is an inevitable part of any profession, but it is crucial for mentors to recognize its impact and take proactive steps to manage it effectively. By managing stress, mentors can maintain their own well-being and provide the support and guidance student teachers need.

Mentors must prioritize self-care to ensure their physical, mental, and emotional well-being. Engaging in activities that promote relaxation, such as exercise, hobbies, or spending time with loved ones, can help alleviate stress and rejuvenate the mind and body.

Effective time management is essential for maintaining a healthy work-life balance. Mentors should prioritize tasks, set realistic goals, and delegate responsibilities when possible. Creating a schedule that allows for breaks and downtime can prevent overwhelming workloads and promote a sense of control.

Setting clear boundaries between work and personal life is crucial for preventing burnout. Mentors should establish limits on working hours, resist the temptation to bring work home, and create a supportive network of colleagues or friends who can offer guidance and understanding.

Mentors should not hesitate to seek support when feeling overwhelmed. Collaborating with colleagues, sharing experiences and challenges, and seeking advice from mentors' networks can provide valuable insights and encouragement.

Engaging in reflective practice allows mentors to process their experiences, identify areas for improvement, and develop strategies for personal and professional growth. Journaling, participating in professional development activities, or seeking supervision from experienced mentors can enhance self-awareness and prevent burnout.

Open and honest communication is essential in managing stress. Mentors should feel comfortable discussing concerns, challenges, and workload with their colleagues or supervisors. Sharing thoughts and feelings can alleviate stress and provide opportunities for support and collaboration.

Practicing mindfulness techniques, such as deep breathing exercises or meditation, can help mentors stay present in the moment, reduce stress, and promote overall well-being. Taking a few minutes each day to focus on the present can cultivate a sense of calm and clarity.

Recognizing and celebrating achievements, both big and small, can boost morale and motivation. Mentors should take time to acknowledge their own accomplishments and those of the student teachers they support. Celebrating successes helps maintain a positive outlook and reinforces the impact of their mentoring efforts.

7.2 Building a Support Network

THE ROLE OF A MENTOR requires providing guidance, support, and expertise to help student teachers navigate the complexities of the profession. However, mentors also need support to enhance their own professional growth and well-being.

One of the first steps in building a support network is establishing positive relationships with colleagues. Engaging in professional collaboration and sharing experiences with fellow educators can provide mentors with a sense of camaraderie and create opportunities for learning and growth. Mentors can engage in peer observations, participate in professional learning communities, or attend conferences and workshops to connect with colleagues who share their interests and challenges.

Joining mentorship communities or organizations can provide mentors with a platform to connect with other experienced mentors. These communities offer opportunities for sharing best practices, discussing challenges, and seeking advice from seasoned professionals. Engaging in mentorship communities allows mentors to learn from others' experiences, gain new perspectives, and stay updated with current trends in mentoring and education.

Actively participating in professional development activities is crucial for building a support network. Attending workshops, conferences, and seminars not only enhances mentors' knowledge and skills but also provides opportunities to network with other educators. These events often facilitate collaboration, allowing mentors to share their expertise and gain insights from a diverse group of professionals.

The digital age has provided educators with the opportunity to connect and collaborate virtually. Joining online communities, such as educational forums, social media groups, or mentorship platforms, can be a convenient way for mentors to build a support network. These platforms enable mentors to share resources, ask questions, and engage in discussions with educators from around the world.

Mentoring circles are small groups of mentors who meet regularly to discuss their experiences, challenges, and successes. These circles provide a safe and supportive environment for mentors to share their thoughts and concerns, seek advice, and receive feedback. Mentoring circles foster a sense of belonging and collaboration, allowing mentors to learn from one another and grow collectively.

Building a support network also involves establishing a positive relationship with school administrators. Engaging in open and regular communication with administrators ensures that mentors receive the necessary support and resources to effectively fulfill their mentoring responsibilities. Administrators can provide guidance, address concerns, and recognize the valuable contributions mentors make to the school community.

Hello again, Dear Reader,

As we reach the end of our mentoring journey, I want to take a moment to express my deepest gratitude for joining me on this transformative path. Together, we have explored the intricate art of mentoring, uncovering its power to shape the lives of student teachers and create lasting change in the realm of education.

Throughout this book, we have delved into the essential elements of effective mentoring. We have discussed the importance of understanding the role of a mentor, setting clear goals and expectations, and establishing a positive and supportive mentoring relationship. We have explored strategies for supporting student teacher development, addressing challenges, fostering inclusion, and navigating ethical considerations. We have delved into the realms of assessment and evaluation, self-care, and personal growth.

But our journey doesn't end here. In fact, it is just the beginning. As mentors, our impact extends far beyond the pages of this book. We have the power to shape the future of education by guiding, inspiring, and uplifting the next generation of educators. The knowledge and insights gained from our shared experience will continue to resonate in the classrooms where our student teachers thrive.

As you reflect on the moments of growth, connection, and transformation that have unfolded during our journey, I encourage you to carry them forward into your own mentoring practice. Embrace the lessons learned, the challenges overcome, and the successes celebrated. Let them serve as a reminder of the profound influence you possess as a mentor and the tremendous difference you make in the lives of your mentees.

Remember, mentoring is a continuous and evolving process. It requires ongoing dedication, reflection, and learning. Seek opportunities to refine your skills, expand your knowledge, and deepen your understanding of the ever-changing landscape of education. Embrace the joy of being a lifelong learner, for it is through our own growth that we inspire growth in others.

As we part ways, I want to express my heartfelt appreciation for your commitment to mentoring and your unwavering dedication to the field of education. Your passion, compassion, and enthusiasm make a world of difference, not only in the lives of your student teachers but also in the broader educational community.

I encourage you to cherish the memories and connections forged throughout this mentoring journey. Hold on to the moments of inspiration and the profound impact you have had on the lives of those you have mentored. Your legacy as a mentor will continue to shine brightly, igniting the spark of greatness in generations of educators to come.

Thank you for embarking on this mentoring adventure with me. May your journey be filled with purpose, fulfillment, and the joy of witnessing the transformative power of mentoring.

With deep appreciation,

Cheryl.

Further Reading

Podsen, India J., and Denmark, Vicki. *Coaching and Mentoring First-Year and Student Teachers*. United Kingdom, Taylor & Francis, 2013.

Portner, Hal. *Mentoring New Teachers*. United Kingdom, SAGE Publications, 2008.

Weisling, Nina F., and Gardiner, Wendy. *Responsive Mentoring: Supporting the Teachers All Students Deserve*. United States, Rowman & Littlefield Publishers, 2020.

Wetzel, Melissa Mosley, et al. *Mentoring Preservice Teachers Through Practice: A Framework for Coaching with CARE*. United Kingdom, Taylor & Francis, 2017.

Don't miss out!

Visit the website below and you can sign up to receive emails whenever Cheryl Angst publishes a new book. There's no charge and no obligation.

https://books2read.com/r/B-A-SBAY-FCYJC

BOOKS 2 READ

Connecting independent readers to independent writers.

About the Author

Cheryl Angst has been teaching in the classroom for over twenty-five years. With a Masters in curriculum and instruction, her passion centers around finding tips, tricks, and strategies to enhance her practice.

Cheryl is a firm believer that learning should be fun for both the students and the teacher. If it isn't engaging, or doesn't spark joy, it's likely able to be done differently.

The "Quick Reads for Busy Educators" series is designed to maximize the precious time educators have. Each book is short enough to be read in an hour or less, but contains a wealth of information on the topic. Some books are overviews of strategies and approaches (enough to help educators decide if it's for them) and some are deeper dives into specific aspects of those larger approaches. This allows busy educators to grab the information they need quickly and efficiently.

If there's a topic you'd like to see covered in the "Quick Reads" series, please let us know!